Mathematics Vocabulary CHALLENGE 2

William Hartley

TarquinGroup
www.tarquingroup.com

William Hartley is the author of some forty primary maths and science resource books.
He has over 20 years teaching experience in both primary and secondary classrooms but now spends his time working as an educational consultant and as a freelance writer of books and interactive online material. He also works as an occasional supply teacher. For relaxation he enjoys ornithology, motor sport and working as a volunteer countryside ranger.

Bullet Points for Teachers or Parents

• A simple way to find out if the vocabulary of a particular worksheet is suitable for a particular class or child is to look at the answers on pages 41 & 42.

• The Vocabulary Check List on page 4 shows which words have been included in the worksheets and also lists a selection of other words which should be known by age 11.

• The worksheets are a valuable resource for homework assignments and it is worth considering also giving each child a photocopy of the Vocabulary Check List on page 4.

• To encourage the renewed interest in accurate spelling, six spelling tests using the key words are given on page 44. Others could easily be constructed.

• Inside the back cover there is a statement of the structure of the UK National Curriculum for Mathematics and the place of this book within it.

• Encourage the use of dictionaries, encyclopedias and other reference material so that the meanings of unfamiliar words can be looked up immediately.

• Use the photocopiable individual record sheet on page 43 for each child to record which worksheets have been done and the scores obtained.

Tarquin
Suite 74, 17 Holywell Hill,
St Albans, AL1 1DT, UK
www.tarquingroup.com

© 2010 William Hartley
ISBN 978 1 89961 891 0
Design: William Hartley
Cover: Jane Adams
Printed in the USA   Distributed in the USA by IPG www.ipgbooks.com

Contents

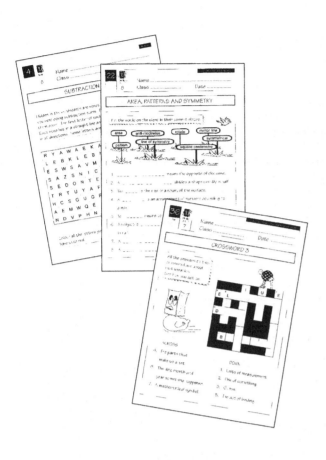

Mathematics Vocabulary Checklist for Key Stage 2

Included in Worksheets 1 - 12: Number

abacus, add, addition, algebra, altogether, answer, approximation, arithmetic, average, bill, borrow, button, buy, cash, change, check, cheque, calculator, coin, column, consecutive, count, currency, decrease, denominator, digital, display, divide, dividend, division, divisor, double, dozen, eighth, equals, equals key, equation, estimate, even, expenses, factor, fewer, fewest, first, fraction, greater than, gross, half, increase, key, last, less than, magic square, mean, memory key, minus, money, more, more than, most, multiple, multiplication, multiplied, narrow, nearest, negative, ninth, notation, number, number bond, number sentence, number-key, number-line, number pattern, numerator, odd, once, owe, payment, pence, percentage, place value, pound, price, product, profit, quarter, quotient, random, receipt, remainder, rounding, salary, same, savings, score, sequence, share equally, sign, spend, subtract, subtraction, symbol, tables, take away, tally, third, times, total, twice, value, wage, zero.

Additional recommended words
accurate, alternate, billion, digit, discount, compare, dollar, equivalent, euro, expensive, fifth, formula, fourth, interest, lend, less, lowest and highest common multiple, million, plus, predict, proportion, row, save, second, sell, seventh, sixth, tenth, treble.

Included in Worksheets 13 -30: Shape, space and measures

a.m. acceleration, acre, acute, after, angle, anti-clockwise, apex, arbitrary unit, area, balance, base, bearing, bisector, border, boundary, celsius, centimetre, circle, co-ordinates, compass, compasses, cone, corner, cube, cubic centimetres, cubic metres, cubit, cuboid, cylinder, day, decimetre, deep, degree, diagonal, direction, distance, east, edge, empty, equilateral triangle, face, fahrenheit, fills, flat, foot, gallon, geometry, gradient, gram, grams, heavy, height, hexagon, hexagonal prism, horizontal, inch, intersect, irregular prism, irregular shape, isosceles triangle, kilogram, kilometres, large, leap year, least, left, length, light, line of symmetry, litres, long, mass, measured, measurement, metre, metre ruler, metric units, middle, midnight, mile, millilitre, millimetre, minute, mirror line, month, multiplication square, network, noon, north, north-east, north-west, obtuse, octagon, ounce, p.m. .parallel, parallelogram, pattern, pentagon, perimeter, pint, plane shape, polygon, pound(mass), prism, protractor, pyramid, quarts, radius, reach, rectangle, reflex, regular polygon, right, rotate, ruler, scale, scalene, scales, set square, shallow, shape, short, sides, size, slope, small, solid, south, south-east, south-west, space, span, speed, sphere, spring balance, square, square centimetre, straight, stride, symmetrical, tall, tape measure, tessellate, today, tomorrow, ton, tonne, trapezium, triangle, triangular, triangular prism, trundle wheel, turn, velocity, vertex, vertical, vertices, volume, week, weigh, weight, yard, year, yesterday.

Additional recommended words
analogue clock, backwards, before, decade, deceleration, digital clock, circumference, forwards, full, hectare, millennium, perpendicular, quadrilateral, sometimes, surface, timer, timetable.

Included in Worksheets 31-36: Handling data and other mathematical words

accuracy, apparatus, arc, axes, bar chart, bar line, between, block graph, bracket, capacity, chart, clockwise, co-ordinates, curved, data, date, deep, difference, elements, equilateral, estimate, exactly, few, fifth, flow charts, function keys, graph, group, guess, high, histogram, horizontal, imperial, inside, less, loan, low, outside, palindrome, perpendicular, pictogram, picture, pie chart, rearrange, spiral, square corner, statistic, tetrahedron, thin, unit, vertical, west, wide.

Additional recommended words
anti-clockwise, biased, classify, database, increasing, information, improbable, interval, median, metric, possibility, probability, questionnaire, survey, tree diagram, uncertain.

Name ....

Class .... Date ....

CALCULATOR WORDS

Look at these words.
Some of them are connected with calculators.
Some of them are not.
Sort out the words and write each one on
the most suitable chart.

| display | magic square | button | consecutive |

| gross | nearest | memory key | most |

| digital | number key | fewer | equals key |

Words connected with calculators	Words not connected with calculators

2	
Mark	Out of
	10

Name ....

Class .... Date ....

THE FOUR RULES OF NUMBER

Choose a word from the list and put it into the right sentence.

multiplication	product	division
take away	Addition	number bond
Subtraction	tables	quotient increase

1. The _ _ _ _ _ _ _ is the answer to a

   _ _ _ _ _ _ _ _ _ _ _ _ _ _ sum.

2. To _ _ _ _ _ _ _ _ something is the same as to remove it.

3. It helps to do multiplication sums if you know your _ _ _ _ _ _

4. To _ _ _ _ _ _ _ _ is to make greater in size or amount.

5. The _ _ _ _ _ _ _ _ is the answer to a _ _ _ _ _ _ _ _ sum.

6. Looking for a _ _ _ _ _ _ _ _ _ _ helps when we add figures.

7. _ _ _ _ _ _ _ _ means something added.

8. _ _ _ _ _ _ _ _ _ _ means something taken away.

KS2 Maths Vocabulary CHALLENGE

Name ....

Class ....   Date ....

ADDITION WORDS

Catch the floating words and put them in their correct places.

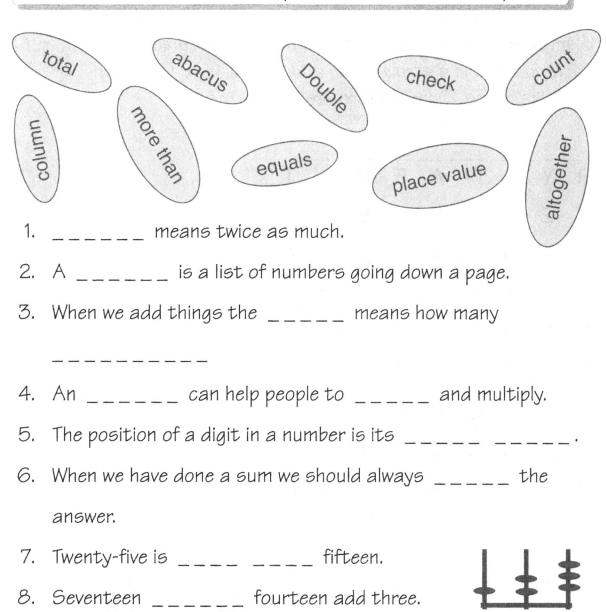

1. _ _ _ _ _ _ means twice as much.

2. A _ _ _ _ _ _ is a list of numbers going down a page.

3. When we add things the _ _ _ _ _ means how many

    _ _ _ _ _ _ _ _ _

4. An _ _ _ _ _ _ can help people to _ _ _ _ _ and multiply.

5. The position of a digit in a number is its _ _ _ _ _ _ _ _ _ _ .

6. When we have done a sum we should always _ _ _ _ _ _ the

    answer.

7. Twenty-five is _ _ _ _ _ _ _ _ fifteen.

8. Seventeen _ _ _ _ _ _ fourteen add three.

4		Name ....
Mark	Out of	Class .... Date ....
	8	

SUBTRACTION WORDS

Hidden in the wordsearch are words that you might use if you were doing subtraction sums. Find the words and write them down. The first letter of each word is given as a clue. Each word lies in a straight line and you will have to search in all directions. Some letters are used twice.

R	Y	A	W	A	E	K	A	T
L	E	B	K	L	E	B	N	C
E	S	W	S	A	V	M	U	A
S	A	Z	S	N	I	C	M	R
S	E	D	O	N	T	E	B	T
T	R	T	U	Y	A	F	E	B
H	C	S	G	U	G	R	R	U
A	E	M	W	Q	E	I	J	S
N	D	V	P	H	N	X	A	C

1. D _ _ _ _ _ _ _

2. A _ _ _ _ _

3. S _ _ _ _ _ _ _

4. L _ _ _ T _ _ _

5. N _ _ _ _ _

6. T _ _ _ A _ _ _

7. M _ _ _ _ _

8. N _ _ _ _ _ _ _

Colour all the letters you have used red.

Colour all the letters you have not used blue.

Name ....

Class ....   Date ....

Mark

Out of

5

10

MULTIPLICATION WORDS

The underlined words are in the wrong sentences.
Sort them out and write the most suitable word
opposite the correct sentence number in the box provided.

1.	4a.	6.
2.	4b.	7.
3.	5.	8.
		9.

1. Nineteen is <u>times</u> than fourteen.

2. Two times six is the <u>Twice</u> as six times two.

3. A ruler can often be used as a <u>dozen</u>.

4. Three <u>multiples</u> four is twelve and four <u>once</u> by six is twenty-four.

5. A <u>symbol</u> eggs means twelve eggs.

6. One time and no more is <u>number-line</u>.

7. Eight and twelve are <u>more</u> of two and four.

8. <u>multiplied</u> means two times.

9. A sign which stands for a number or letter is called a <u>same</u>.

6

Mark

Out of
9

Name ....

Class ....   Date ....

DIVISION WORDS

Read the passage and write in the correct missing words from the list.

A division sum is a _ _ _ _ _ _   _ _ _ _ _ _ _ _ .

If you can _ _ _ _ _   _ _ _ _ _ _ _ you will not have a

_ _ _ _ _ _ _ _ _

The _ _ _ _ _ _ _ _ is the number being divided.

The _ _ _ _ _ _ _ is the number you are dividing by.

Dividing a number by two will give you _ _ _ _ that number.

Dividing a number by four will give you a _ _ _ _ _ _ _ of the

number.

Dividing by three will give you a _ _ _ _ _ and dividing by nine

will give you a _ _ _ _ _ .

share equally	divisor	remainder
number sentence	quarter	third
dividend	half	ninth

Name ....

Class ....   Date ....

FRACTION OR NOT?

Look at the words below.
Some of them are to do with fractions.
Some of them are not.
Sort them out and write each word in the correct column on the chart.

quarter   coin   random   denominator

eighth   algebra   calculator   half

narrow   percentage   estimate   numerator

Words to do with fractions	Words not to do with fractions

Mark	Out of
8	9

Name ....

Class ....   Date ....

USEFUL WORDS 1

Choose the correct word from the list and put it in the right sentence.

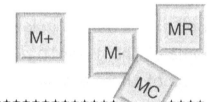

★ ★

divide	rounding	zero
memory keys	first	approximation
greater than	last	number pattern

★ ★

1. Twenty-seven is _ _ _ _ _ _ _ _ _ _ _ _ twenty-six.

2. M+, M-, MR and MC are all _ _ _ _ _ _ _ _ _ _ on a calculator.

3. A _ _ _ _ _ _ _ _ _ _ _ _ _ _ is an arrangement of numbers according to a rule.

4. To get two we would _ _ _ _ _ _ twelve by six.

5. When counting from one to twenty, one is the _ _ _ _ _ and twenty is the _ _ _ _ .

6. Another name for 'nought' is _ _ _ _ .

7. An _ _ _ _ _ _ _ _ _ _ _ _ _ is a guess that is nearly correct.

8. Writing a number to the nearest ten is called _ _ _ _ _ _ _ _ .

Name ....

Class .... Date ....

MONEY WORDS

Catch the floating words and put them in their correct places.

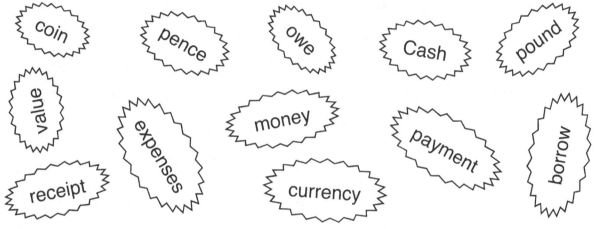

coin   pence   owe   Cash   pound

value   expenses   money   payment   borrow

receipt   currency

1. _ _ _ _ is a word that means paper money and coins.

2. What you spend is known as your _ _ _ _ _ _ _ _ .

3. The amount that _ _ _ _ _ is worth is known as it's _ _ _ _ _ .

4. Another name for money is _ _ _ _ _ _ _ _ .

5. A five _ _ _ _ _ _ _ _ _ is not worth as much as a _ _ _ _ _ _ .

6. A tradesperson will give you a _ _ _ _ _ _ _ as proof

    of _ _ _ _ _ _ _ .

7. When you _ _ _ somebody money you have a duty to pay them.

8. Sometimes we _ _ _ _ _ _ money to buy something.

10	
Mark	Out of
	8

Name ....

Class ....   Date ....

PAYING IN, PAYING OUT!

In the wordsearch are eight words to do with earning, saving and spending money.
Find them and write them down.
The first letter of each word is given as a clue.
You will have to search in all directions.
Some letters are used twice.

1. s _ _ _ _ _ _

2. s _ _ _ _

3. p _ _ _ _ _

4. s _ _ _ _ _

5. b _ _ _

6. w _ _ _

7. p _ _ _ _

8. b _ _

m	c	x	o	e	b	u	y
b	p	r	o	f	i	t	r
f	r	y	n	s	l	q	b
w	i	g	r	d	l	j	d
d	c	e	g	a	w	c	n
h	e	a	a	t	l	y	e
v	i	u	k	z	l	a	p
p	s	g	n	i	v	a	s

Colour all the letters you have used green.

Colour all the letters you have not used yellow.

Name ....

Class ....   Date ....

USEFUL WORDS 2

The underlined words are in the wrong sentences.
Sort them out and write the most suitable word
opposite the correct sentence number in the box provided.

1. A Tally is an order to a bank to pay money.

2. A set of numbers written in order is a cheque.

3. Arithmetic marks show a record of the score.

4. A fraction is an electronic machine for performing mathematical calculations.

5. Each rule of number has it's own calculator.

6. The sequence of two, four and six is four.

7. Twenty items is called a change.

8. Sign involves dealing with numbers.

9. If you tender more money than the item costs you will get some score.

10. A average is a part of something.

1.	
2.	
3.	
4.	
5.	
6.	
7.	
8.	
9.	
10.	

Mark	Out of
	9

Name ....

Class .... Date ....

CROSSWORD 1

All the answers to this crossword are about mathematics.
See how you get on.

1 F
2 O
3 M
4 N
5 A
6 E
T
7 K
8 F
T
9 E
T
N

ACROSS

3. A type of average.
5. Short for 'addition'.
8. The least number.
9. A type of mathematical sum that balances.

DOWN

1. A number that divides exactly into another number.
2. Not even.
4. The way mathematical statements are written.
6. Not odd.
7. A button on a keyboard.

Name ....

Class ....   Date ....

2D or 3D?

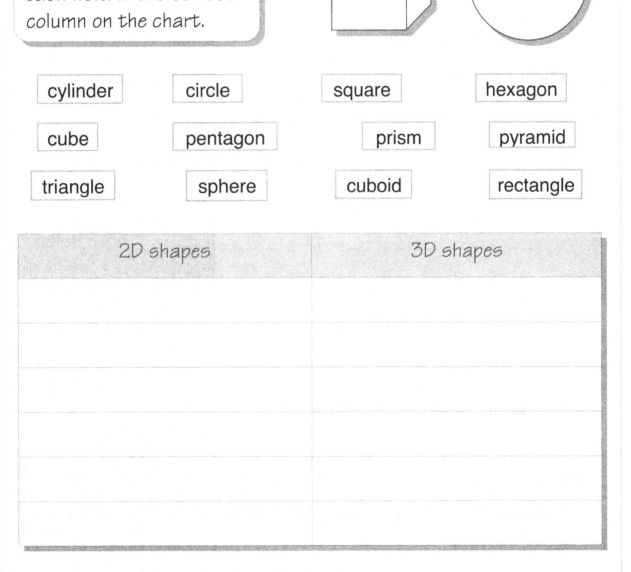

Look at the names of the 2D and 3D shapes below. Sort them out and write each word in the correct column on the chart.

cylinder   circle   square   hexagon

cube   pentagon   prism   pyramid

triangle   sphere   cuboid   rectangle

2D shapes	3D shapes

14

Mark | Out of
10

Name ....

Class .... Date ....

2D (PLANE) SHAPES

Choose the best word from the list for each of these sentences.

1. A _ _ _ _ _ _ _ _ _ _ is a two-dimensional object.

2. A two-dimensional shape is _ _ _ _ .

3. Some plane shapes will _ _ _ _ _ _ _ _ _ _ but some will not.

4. A _ _ _ _ _ _ is a point where two lines meet.

5. An _ _ _ _ _ _ _ _ _ _ _ _ _ _ _ _ _ _ _ has all sides the

   same length.

6. A _ _ _ _ _ _ _ _ _ _ _ _ _ and a _ _ _ _ _ _ _ _ _ both have

   four sides.

7. An _ _ _ _ _ _ _ has eight _ _ _ _ _ .

8. An _ _ _ _ _ _ _ _ _ _ _ _ _ _ _ _

   has two sides the same length.

```
★★★★★★★★★★★★★★★★★★★★★★★★★★★★★★★★★★★★★★★★★★★★★★★★★
★   tessellate  corner  octagon  equilateral triangle  plane shape   ★
★       isosceles triangle  parallelogram  sides  flat  trapezium     ★
★★★★★★★★★★★★★★★★★★★★★★★★★★★★★★★★★★★★★★★★★★★★★★★★★
```

Name ....

Class ....   Date ....

Mark | Out of
15 | 10

3D (SOLID) SHAPES

Catch the floating words and put them in their correct places.

triangular prism   shape   hexagonal prism   vertices   cone   diagonal   irregular prism   base   face   vertex

1. The b _ _ _ is the bottom part on which a thing rests.

2. The base is also a f _ _ _ of a solid geometric figure.

3. The plural of v _ _ _ _ _ is v _ _ _ _ _ _ _ .

4. A line across a shape from one corner to another is called a

    d _ _ _ _ _ _ _ .

5. A t _ _ _ _ _ _ _ _ _ p _ _ _ _ has a front face that is a

    triangle.

6. An i _ _ _ _ _ _ _ _ p _ _ _ _ has a front face with no

    particular s _ _ _ _ .

7. The front face of a h _ _ _ _ _ _ _ _ p _ _ _ _ is a hexagon.

8. A c _ _ _ is a solid with a pointed top and a circular base.

16

Mark | Out of
9

Name ....

Class .... Date ....

ALL SORTS OF WORDS 1

The words in capital letters are in the wrong sentences.
Sort them out and write the most suitable word
opposite the correct sentence number in the box provided.

1.	
2.	
3.	
4.	
5.	
6.	
7.	
8.	
9.	

1. Incline is another word for TRIANGULAR.

2. SLOPE is another name for speed.

3. Two lines the same distance apart
   are SMALL.

4. A plane shape bounded by three
   straight lines is LARGE.

5. PARALLEL things are little in size.

6. VELOCITY things are big in size.

7. The study of shapes is called
   POLYGON.

8. A plane shape bounded by straight
   lines is a BORDER.

9. Another name for GEOMETRY is edge.

Name ....

Class .... Date ....

ALL SORTS OF WORDS 2

In the wordsearch are eight words to do with shape, space and measures.
Clues and first letters are given to help you find them. Each word lies in a straight line and you will have to search in all directions. Some letters are used twice.

1. Centre. M

2. Slope. G

3. Straight up and down. V

4. Not hollow. S

5. Not short. T

6. Border. E

7. Measurement of liquid. G

8. The smallest in size. L

V	I	T	S	A	E	L	T
E	T	B	O	O	J	A	N
R	E	P	L	G	L	C	E
T	H	G	I	L	D	U	I
I	M	I	D	D	L	E	D
C	N	A	R	E	Q	K	A
A	V	F	M	S	W	E	R
L	L	N	O	L	L	A	G

Mark each word with a line in a different colour.

18

Mark | Out of
9

Name ....

Class .... Date ....

THE BEST TOOL FOR THE JOB

Read the sentences and then choose the number of the most suitable listed word and write it in the brackets at the end of each question.

1. To measure a long distance outside I would use a **?** (___)

2. To help with multiplication sums I would use a **?** (___)

3. I would use a **?** to measure angles. (___)

4. I would use a **?** or a **?** to find the width of the classroom.

   (___) (___)

5. I would use **?** to find the mass of an object. (___)

6. I would use a pair of **?** to draw circles. (___)

7. I would use a **?** for finding right angles. (___)

8. I could use an **?** if no standard measuring tool was available.

   (___)

4 scales	5 trundle wheel	9 multiplication square
8 arbitrary unit	2 protractor	3 compasses
7 metre rule	6 set square	1 tape measure

Name ....

Class ....   Date ....

19

Mark

Out of

12

IMPERIAL OR METRIC?

At the bottom of the page are the names of some measuring units. Decide if they belong to the imperial or the metric measuring system. Then write the sorted words in the correct column on the chart.

Imperial unit	Metric unit

ton   kilogram   yard   centimetre

metre   ounce   tonne   gram

millimetre   inch   mile   pound (mass)

20

Mark | Out of
8

Name ....

Class .... Date ....

LENGTH

Choose the correct word from the list for each of these sentences.

★★★★★★★★★★★★★★★★★
kilometres
short
distance
perimeter
decimetre
cubit
Long
stride
★★★★★★★★★★★★★★★★★

1. The _ _ _ _ _ _ _ _ is the space between two places or things.

2. _ _ _ _ means to stretch for a considerable distance.

3. Something with not much length is _ _ _ _ _ .

4. A _ _ _ _ _ _ _ _ _ is one tenth of a metre.

5. A long step measured from heel to heel is called a _ _ _ _ _ _ .

6. Road distances in France are measured in _ _ _ _ _ _ _ _ _ _ .

7. From your elbow to your outstretched finger tip is a

_ _ _ _ _ long.

8. The distance round a closed shape is the _ _ _ _ _ _ _ _ _ .

Name ....

Class ....   Date ....

21

Mark | Out of
8

ANGLES AND DIRECTION

In the wordsearch are the names of different types of angle and some words connected with direction.
Find the words and write them down.
The first letter of each word is given as a clue.
Each word lies in a straight line and you will have to search in all directions. Some letters are used twice.

a	e	s	u	t	b	o	t
n	a	o	h	c	d	h	h
h	s	u	t	o	g	r	g
t	t	t	j	i	e	e	i
r	i	h	a	f	k	p	r
o	b	r	l	q	r	a	u
n	t	e	m	v	w	l	s
s	x	f	a	c	u	t	e

1. a _ _ _ _

2. r _ _ _ _

3. s _ _ _ _ _ _ _

4. o _ _ _ _ _

5. r _ _ _ _ _

6. s _ _ _ _

7. n _ _ _ _

8. e _ _ _

Colour all the letters you have used orange.

Colour all the letters you have not used violet.

22

Mark | Out of
8

Name ....

Class .... Date ....

AREA, PATTERNS AND SYMMETRY

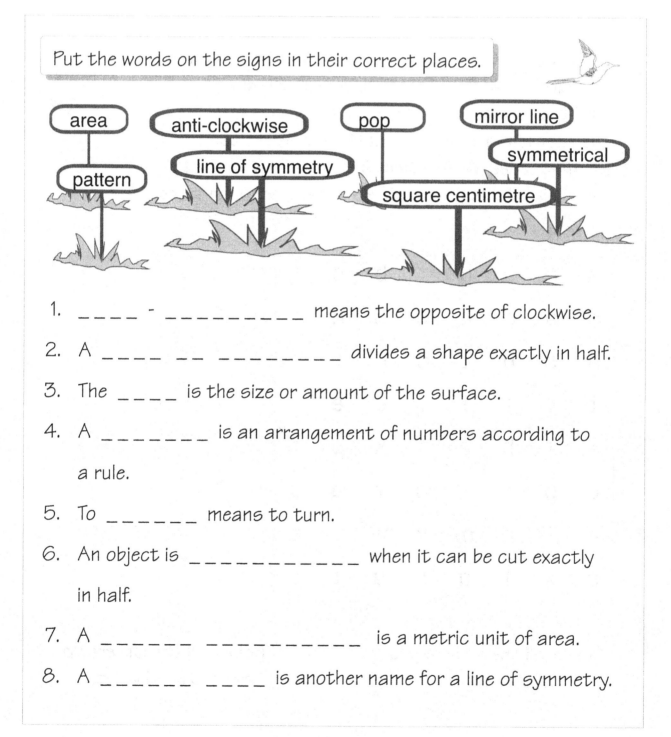

Put the words on the signs in their correct places.

area

anti-clockwise

pop

mirror line

line of symmetry

symmetrical

pattern

square centimetre

1. _ _ _ _ _ - _ _ _ _ _ _ _ _ _ _ means the opposite of clockwise.

2. A _ _ _ _ _ _ _ _ _ _ _ _ _ _ _ divides a shape exactly in half.

3. The _ _ _ _ is the size or amount of the surface.

4. A _ _ _ _ _ _ _ is an arrangement of numbers according to a rule.

5. To _ _ _ _ _ _ means to turn.

6. An object is _ _ _ _ _ _ _ _ _ _ _ _ when it can be cut exactly in half.

7. A _ _ _ _ _ _ _ _ _ _ _ _ _ _ _ _ is a metric unit of area.

8. A _ _ _ _ _ _ _ _ _ _ is another name for a line of symmetry.

Name ....

Class ....   Date ....

23

Mark | Out of
10

MASS

> The underlined words are in the wrong sentences.
> Sort them out and write the most suitable word
> opposite the correct sentence number in the box provided.

1. Scales are used to <u>weight</u> material.

2. The <u>weigh</u> of something tells you how heavy it is.

3. Things that are <u>spring balance</u> are difficult to lift.

4. A <u>kilogram</u> is a weighing machine with a hook on one end.

5. Items that are <u>heavy</u> are easier to lift.

6. A <u>balance</u> is lighter than a tonne.

7. A kilogram is equal to a 1000 <u>tonne</u>.

8. A <u>light</u> equals a 1000 kilograms.

9. A set of scales is a <u>mass</u>.

10. The <u>grams</u> of something is similar to its weight.

1.	
2.	
3.	
4.	
5.	
6.	
7.	
8.	
9.	
10.	

24

Mark | Out of
| 11

Name ....

Class ....   Date ....

CROSSWORD 2

All the answers to this crossword are about shape, space and measures.

ACROSS

1. In the morning.

2. Top point of a pyramid.

5. To stretch out the hand to get.

7. Makes completely full.

9. Border.

DOWN

1. Area of land.

3. After midday.

4. Triangle with unequal sides.

6. Nothing in it.

7. Measurement of length.

8. Little finger to thumb.

Name ....

Class .... Date ....

ALL SORTS OF WORDS 3

regular polygon

Length

Celsius

Fahrenheit

degree

Acceleration

radius

irregular shape

intersect

Catch the floating words and put them in their correct places.

1. _ _ _ _ l _ _ _ _ _ _ _ _ is an increase in speed.

2. When two roads cross they _ _ _ _ r _ _ _ _ .

3. A r _ _ _ _ _ _ p _ _ _ _ _ _ has sides the same length and equal angles.

4. _ _ _ s _ _ _ and _ _ _ _ _ _ h _ _ _ are names for scales of temperature.

5. A _ _ _ _ e _ is a scale mark on a thermometer or an angle measurement.

6. L _ _ _ _ _ is the distance something measures from end to end.

7. An _ _ _ _ g _ _ _ _ _ _ a _ _ has sides and angles that are not equal.

8. The distance from the centre of a circle to the edge is the _ _ _ _ u _ .

26

Mark | Out of
9

Name ....

Class .... Date ....

ALL SORTS OF WORDS 4

The missing words for these sentences are listed but their letters are all mixed-up. Rearrange the letters and write the number of the most suitable word in the brackets at the end of each sentence. The first letter of each word has been written in capital letters.

1. **?** is finding out the size or weight of something. (___)

2. When two lines meet an **?** forms between them. (___)

3. The **?** on a map tells you how distance and size are shown.

(___)

4. **?** means laying flat. (___)

5. There are three hundred and sixty-five days in a **?** (___)

6. If something is **?** it is not deep. (___)

7. **?** and **?** are points of the compass. (___) (___)

8. To **?** is to revolve or rotate. (___)

9 ooritHznal	1 aScle	3 ureMaesmnet
4 Soahllw	2 uTrn	8 Nohtr-seWt
7 eYar	5 nAegl	6 thNro-tEas

Name ....

Class .... Date ....

TIME AND TIME AGAIN!

Read the clues on the left, sort out the words in the middle and write them in their correct places in the column on the right.

Clue	Word	Correct order
1. This day.	tomorrow	1. _____
2. A longer year.	yesterday	2. _____
3. One sixtieth of an hour.	day	3. _____
4. End of the day.	noon	4. _____
5. The day before today.	minute	5. _____
6. $\frac{1}{7}$ of a week.	today	6. _____
7. The day after today.	leap year	7. _____
8. Twelve in a year.	after	8. _____
9. Not before.	midnight	9. _____
10. 12 o' clock midday.	months	10. _____

28

Mark | Out of
11

Name ....

Class ....   Date ....

VOLUME AND CAPACITY

Choose the most suitable word from the list and put it in the right sentence.

litres	Volume	cubic centimetres	Large	deep	quarts

measured	metric units	space	cubic metres	millilitre

1. _ _ _ u _ _ is the _ p _ _ _ taken up by something.

2. Small volumes are measured in _ _ _ _ c _ _ _ _ _ _ m _ _ _ _ _ _ .

3. L _ _ _ _ volumes are measured in _ _ b _ _ _ e _ _ _ _ .

4. A _ _ _ _ i _ _ _ _ _ is a very small volume of liquid.

5. Milk, lemonade and petrol are usually _ _ _ _ u _ _ _ in

    _ i _ _ _ _ .

6. A _ _ e _ container will hold more liquid than a shallow one.

7. Millilitres, centilitres and litres are all _ _ _ r _ _ u _ _ _ _ .

8. Pints, gallons, fluid ounces and _ _ a _ _ _ are all imperial

    units.

Name ....

Class ....   Date ....

WHICH DIRECTION?

Choose the most suitable word from the boxes and write it in the correct sentence.

★★★★★★★★★★★★★★★★★★
★ South-west ★
★ direction ★
★ Co-ordinates ★
★★★★★★★★★★★★★★★★★★

1. The opposite of _ _ _ _ is right.

2. A _ _ _ _ _ _ _ _ needle points towards the magnetic _ _ _ _ _ _ .

3. _ _ _ _ _ - _ _ _ _ is midway between south and west.

4. _ _ _ _ _ - _ _ _ _ is midway between south and east.

5. The opposite of _ _ _ _ _ is left.

6. The clockwise angle between the north line and the line to an object is known as the _ _ _ _ _ _ _ .

7. Something that is not crooked is _ _ _ _ _ _ _ _ .

8. The line or course along which you move is called your _ _ _ _ _ _ _ _ _ .

9. _ _ - _ _ _ _ _ _ _ _ _ are two numbers which show a point on a graph or grid.

★★★
★ left   right   north   compass   bearing   straight ★
★★

30

Mark | Out of

8

Name ....

Class ....   Date ....

ASSORTED WORDS WORDSEARCH

1. Cuts in half. B

2. Measurement
   for liquid. P

3. Measures
   length. R

4. Quickness
   of movement. S

5. Connected
   lines. N

6. Seven days. W

7. Length from top
   to bottom. H

8. How big
   something is. S

In this wordsearch are eight words to do with shape, space and measures. Clues and first letters are given to help you find them.
Each word lies in a straight line but you will need to search in all directions.

Rule a line of a different colour over each word.

B	K	R	O	W	T	E	N
N	I	H	X	T	U	V	B
T	W	S	C	O	D	A	I
Y	H	K	E	E	W	A	R
S	D	G	E	C	Z	F	E
L	I	P	I	N	T	R	L
M	S	Z	P	E	G	O	U
E	K	J	E	Q	H	S	R

Name ....

Class ....   Date ....

HANDLING DATA 1

Catch the floating words and put them in their correct places.

1. A _ _ _ p _ is a picture of numerical information.

2. A _ h _ _ _ gives facts in an easily

   understandable form.

3. When drawing graphs and charts great

   _ _ _ u _ _ _ _ should be shown.

4. D _ _ _ are numbers that have been

   collected for study.

5. A graph usually has two _ x _ _

6. The axes of a graph are _ _ _ _ _ _ c _ _

   and _ _ _ _ z _ _ _ _ _ _

7. The _ o - _ _ _ _ _ _ a _ _ _ tell you where

   the points are on a graph.

8. A _ _ e _ _ _ r _ is a means of showing

   information in a circular layout.

 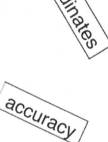

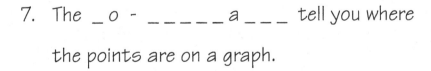
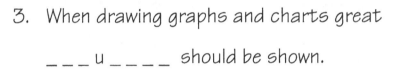
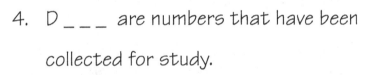

32

Mark | Out of
9

Name ....

Class .... Date ....

HANDLING DATA 2

Choose the most suitable word from the list and put it in the right sentence.

1. A _ a _ _ _ _ _ t and a _ l _ _ _ _ _ a _ _ both use columns to show information.

2. The data is shown by lines on a _ a _ _ _ n _ graph.

3. A _ _ c _ _ _ _ graph and a _ _ _ _ o _ _ _ _ both show facts in picture form.

4. A _ _ _ _ _ _ s _ _ _ is a piece of numerical information.

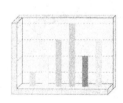

bar chart	statistic	histogram
pictogram	bar line	groups
Flow charts	block graph	picture

5. A bar chart is a form of _ i _ _ _ g _ _ _

6. _ _ _ w _ _ _ r _ _ show the order in which things should happen.

7. Information is often collected into _ _ o u _ _ to show on a chart.

　　KS2 Maths Vocabulary CHALLENGE

Name ....

Class ....   Date ....

Mark | Out of
10

USEFUL WORDS TO KNOW 1

Read the clues on the left. Sort out the mixed-up letters in the middle to make the correct word to put in the column on the right.

Clue	Letters	Correct word
1. Cross at right angles.	aenlpurepdicr	1. _____
2. Unlikeness of two things.	rfdifeence	2. _____
3. Not inside.	osutide	3. _____
4. A right angle.	qsaure ocrenr	4. _____
5. 424 is one.	palnidorme	5. _____
6. Bent without angles.	ucvred	6. _____
7. How much it holds.	cpacatiy	7. _____
8. Not outside.	iisnde	8. _____
9. Precisely.	caextly	9. _____
10. All sides equal.	eailqutreal	10. _____

34

Mark | Out of

8

Name ....

Class ....   Date ....

USEFUL WORDS TO KNOW 2

In this wordsearch are eight mathematical words or phrases. Clues and first letters are given to help you find them. Each word lies in a straight line but you will need to search in all directions.
Draw a line through the letters for each word in a different colour.
Some letters are used twice.

A	R	C	S	S	Y	E	K	N	O	I	T	C	N	U	F
K	V	T	N	S	P	I	R	A	L	H	I	H	X	C	D
R	Y	T	S	E	W	J	G	F	I	F	T	H	B	P	O
U	L	M	A	L	Q	W	F	N	E	E	W	T	E	B	E

1. Buttons on a calculator. (two words)   F. K.

2. Not thick. T

3. Not so much. L

4. Comes after fourth. F

5. In the middle of two things. B

6. A curved line joining two points. A

7. A spring-like curve. S

8. Opposite east. W

Name ....

Class ....   Date ....

35

Mark | Out of
10

USEFUL WORDS TO KNOW 3

The underlined words are in the wrong sentences.
Sort them out and write the most suitable word
opposite the correct sentence number in the box provided.

1. The opposite of shallow is <u>clockwise</u>.

2. If there are not many then there are <u>guess</u>.

3. The hands of a clock travel <u>high</u>.

4. To <u>deep</u> is to put something into a new order.

5. The opposite of <u>few</u> is narrow.

6. Another name for estimate is <u>tetrahedron</u>.

7. The equipment needed is the <u>rearrange</u>.

8. The opposite of <u>apparatus</u> is low.

9. The opposite of <u>wide</u> is high.

10. A <u>low</u> is a solid with four triangular faces.

1.

2.

3.

4.

5.

6.

7.

8.

9.

10.

36

Mark | Out of
7

Name ....

Class .... Date ....

CROSSWORD 3

All the answers to this crossword are about mathematics.
See how you get on.

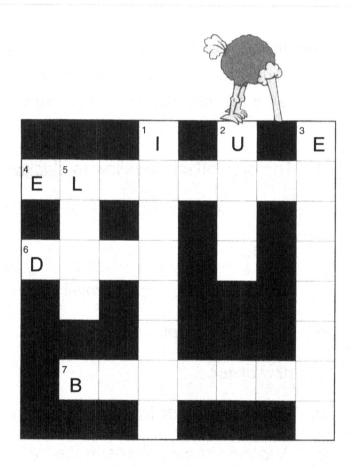

ACROSS

4. The parts that make up a set

6. The day, month and year something happened

7. A mathematical symbol

DOWN

1. Units of measurement

2. One of something

3. Guess

5. The act of lending

1 (in any order) **Words connected with calculators**: memory key, digital, equals key, display, button, number key
Words not connected with calculators: gross, fewer, consecutive, most, nearest, magic square

2 1. product, multiplication 2. take away 3. tables 4. increase 5. quotient, division
6. number bond 7. Addition 8. Subtraction

3 1. Double 2. column 3. total, altogether 4. abacus, count 5. place value 6. check 7. more than
8. equals

4 1. DECREASE 2. ANSWER 3. SUBTRACT 4. LESS THAN 5. NUMBER 6. TAKE AWAY
7. MINUS 8. NEGATIVE   Used letters coloured red. Unused letters coloured blue.

5 1. more 2. same 3. number-line 4a. times 4b. multiplied 5. dozen 6. once 7. multiples
8. Twice 9. symbol

6 (in correct order) number sentence, share equally, remainder, dividend, divisor, half, quarter, third, ninth

7 (in any order) **Words to do with fractions**: quarter, half, percentage, eighth, numerator, denominator,
Words not to do with fractions: coin, algebra, random, calculator, estimate, narrow

8 1. greater than 2. memory keys 3. number pattern 4. divide 5. first, last 6. zero
7. approximation 8. rounding

9 1. Cash 2. expenses 3. money, value 4. currency 5. pence, coin, pound 6. receipt, payment
7. owe 8. borrow

10 1. savings 2. spend 3. profit 4. salary 5. bill 6. wage 7. price 8. buy
Used letters should be coloured green. Unused letters should be coloured yellow.

11 1. cheque 2. sequence 3. Tally 4. calculator 5. sign 6. average 7. score 8. Arithmetic
9. change 10. fraction

12 **Across**: 3. MEAN 5. ADD 8. FEWEST 9. EQUATION
Down: 1. FACTOR 2. ODD 4. NOTATION 6. EVEN 7. KEY

13 (in any order) **2D shapes**: pentagon, rectangle, square, circle, hexagon, triangle
3D shapes: cuboid, prism, pyramid, cylinder, sphere, cube

14 1. plane shape 2. flat 3. tessellate 4. corner 5. equilateral triangle 6. parallelogram, trapezium
7. octagon, sides 8. isosceles triangle

15 1. base 2. face 3. vertex, vertices 4. diagonal 5. triangular prism 6. irregular prism, shape
7. hexagonal prism 8. cone

16 1. SLOPE 2. VELOCITY 3. PARALLEL 4. TRIANGULAR 5. SMALL 6. LARGE
7. GEOMETRY 8. POLYGON 9. BORDER

17 1. MIDDLE 2. GRADIENT 3. VERTICAL 4. SOLID 5. TALL 6. EDGE 7. GALLON 8. LEAST
Each word should be shaded in a different colour.

18 1. 5 2. 9 3. 2 4. (in any order) 1 7 5. 4 6. 3 7. 6 8. 8
1. trundle wheel 2. multiplication square 3. protractor 4. tape measure, metre ruler 5. scales
6. compasses 7. set square 8. arbitrary unit

19 (in any order) **Imperial units**: ton, yard, ounce, mile, inch, pound (mass)
Metric units: kilogram, centimetre, metre, tonne, gram, millimetre

20 1. distance 2. Long 3. short 4. decimetre 5. stride 6. kilometres 7. cubit 8. perimeter

21 1. acute 2. right 3. straight 4. obtuse 5. reflex 6. south 7. north 8. east
Used letters should be coloured orange. Unused letters should be coloured violet.

22 1. Anti-clockwise 2. line of symmetry 3. area 4. pattern 5. rotate 6. symmetrical
7. square centimetre 8. mirror line

23 1. weigh 2. weight 3. heavy 4. spring balance 5. light 6. kilogram 7. grams 8. tonne
9. balance 10. mass

24 **Across**: 1. A.M. 2. APEX 5. REACH 7. FILLS 9. BOUNDARY
Down: 1. ACRE 3. P.M. 4. SCALENE 6. EMPTY 7. FOOT 8. SPAN

25 1. Acceleration 2. intersect 3. regular polygon 4. Celsius, Fahrenheit 5. degree 6. Length
7. irregular shape 8. radius

26 1. 3 2. 5 3. 1 4. 9 5. 7 6. 4 7. (in any order) 6 8 8. 2
1. Measurement 2. angle 3. scale 4. Horizontal 5. year 6. shallow
7. (in any order) North-east, North-west 8. turn

27 1. today 2. leap year 3. minute 4. midnight 5. yesterday 6. day 7. tomorrow 8. months
9. after 10. noon

28 1. Volume, space 2. cubic centimetres 3. Large, cubic metres 4. millilitre 5. measured, litres
6. deep 7. metric units 8. quarts

29 1. left 2. compass, north 3. South-west 4. South-east 5. right 6. bearing 7. straight
8. direction 9. Co-ordinates

30 1. BISECTOR 2. PINT 3. RULER 4. SPEED 5. NETWORK 6. WEEK 7. HEIGHT 8. SIZE
Each word should be shaded in a different colour.

31 1. graph 2. chart 3. accuracy 4. Data 5. axes 6. vertical, horizontal 7. co-ordinates
8. pie chart

32 1. bar chart, block graph 2. bar line 3. picture, pictogram 4. statistic 5. histogram
6. Flow charts 7. groups

33 1. perpendicular 2. difference 3. outside 4. square corner 5. palindrome 6. curved 7. capacity
8. inside 9. exactly 10. equilateral

34 1. FUNCTION KEYS 2. THIN 3. LESS 4. FIFTH 5. BETWEEN 6. ARC 7. SPIRAL 8. WEST
The letters for each word should be shaded the same colour.

35 1. deep 2. few 3. clockwise 4. rearrange 5. wide 6. guess 7. apparatus 8. high 9. low
10. tetrahedron

36 **Across**: 4. ELEMENTS 6. DATE 7. BRACKET
Down: 1. IMPERIAL 2. UNIT 3. ESTIMATE 5. LOAN

Maths Vocabulary CHALLENGE
How Well Have I Done? - Individual Record Sheet

Name _____ Class _____

Sheet	Date	Comments	Mark	Poss Mark	Sheet	Date	Comments	Mark	Poss Mark
1				12	19				12
2				10	20				8
3				10	21				8
4				8	22				8
5				10	23				10
6				9	24				11
7				12	25				9
8				9	26				9
9				12	27				10
10				8	28				11
11				10	29				10
12				9	30				8
13				12	31				9
14				10	32				9
15				10	33				10
16				9	34				8
17				8	35				10
18				9	36				7

Six Spelling Tests

Number

1. multiplication
2. calculator
3. abacus
4. column
5. remainder
6. quotient
7. approximation
8. eighth
9. numerator
10. sequence
11. subtraction
12. rounding
13. symbol
14. payment
15. receipt
16. currency
17. cheque
18. consecutive
19. division
20. fraction

Shape, Space & Measures

1. cylinder
2. hexagon
3. pyramid
4. isosceles
5. rectangle
6. quadrilateral
7. parallelogram
8. diagonal
9. vertices
10. velocity
11. backwards
12. arbitrary
13. trundle wheel
14. compasses
15. millimetre
16. kilogram
17. perimeter
18. protractor
19. perpendicular
20. south-west

Handling Data & General

1. palindrome
2. vertical
3. accuracy
4. pictogram
5. histogram
6. statistic
7. difference
8. capacity
9. anti-clockwise
10. apparatus
11. perpendicular
12. rearrange
13. axes
14. information
15. brackets
16. estimate
17. increasing
18. questionnaire
19. database
20. possibility

Number

1. altogether
2. equals
3. place value
4. denominator
5. tables
6. tally
7. digital
8. expensive
9. euro
10. alternate
11. proportion
12. multiplied
13. notation
14. discount
15. zero
16. magic square
17. fewest
18. equivalent
19. average
20. arithmetic

Shape, Space & Measures

1. bisector
2. co-ordinates
3. celsius
4. tessellate
5. trapezium
6. yesterday
7. circumference
8. spring balance
9. measurement
10. millennium
11. irregular
12. equilateral
13. symmetrical
14. weight
15. height
16. intersect
17. obtuse
18. horizontal
19. triangular
20. acceleration

Handling Data & General

1. clockwise
2. flow charts
3. tetrahedron
4. guess
5. elements
6. between
7. metric
8. imperial
9. fifth
10. improbable
11. block graph
12. pie chart
13. uncertain
14. outside
15. classify
16. exactly
17. probability
18. biased
19. function keys
20. tree diagram